Ecosystems Research Journal

Bamboo Forest Research Journal

Heather C. Hudak

CRABTREE
PUBLISHING COMPANY
WWW.CRABTREEBOOKS.COM

CRABTREE
PUBLISHING COMPANY
WWW.CRABTREEBOOKS.COM

Author: Heather Hudak

Editors: Sonya Newland, Kathy Middleton

Design: Clare Nicholas

Cover design: Abigail Smith

Illustrator: Ron Dixon

Proofreader: Wendy Scavuzzo

Production coordinator and prepress technician: Tammy McGarr

Print coordinator: Katherine Berti

Produced for Crabtree Publishing Company by White-Thomson Publishing

Photo Credits:

Cover: Wikimedia bottom right bird;
All other images from Shutterstock

Interior: Alamy: p. 12b Nature Picture Library, pp. 14–15 ZUMA Press, Inc., pp. 16–17 JTB Media Creation, Inc., pp. 20–21 CWIS, p. 27t MARKA; Getty Images: p. 12t Liu Jin, p. 13 Leisa Tylor; iStock: p. 16l caoyu36, pp. 18–19 caoyu36, p. 25l hejuan, p. 25r badastar, pp. 28–29 hudiemm; Shutterstock: pp. 4–5 Juan He, p. 5t Erni, p. 6t Peter Stuckings, p. 6b Douglas Chiang, p. 7t wannakumpnut, p. 7b 2630ben, pp. 8–9 dailin, p. 9t LP2 Studio, p. 9b ex0rzist, p. 10 LP2 Studio, p. 11t cnyy, p. 11b ronnayut_to, p. 14 Ariyani Tedjo, p. 15t Prasad Khale, p. 15b Luoxi, p. 16r teekayu, p. 17 Hung Chung Chih, p. 18 Bodor Tivadar, p. 19t humphery, p. 20 Analgin, p. 21t beibaoke, p. 21b Wang LiQiang, p. 22 forest71, pp. 22–23 Juan He, p. 23l Plume Photography, p. 23r Wildnerdpix, p. 24l Jesada Sabai, p. 24r lvlinglong, p. 26l Wang LiQiang, p. 26r Super Prin, p. 27b gopause, p. 29t Jamie Farrant, p. 29b Hung Chung Chih.

Library and Archives Canada Cataloguing in Publication

Hudak, Heather C., 1975-, author
        Bamboo forest research journal / Heather Hudak.

(Ecosystems research journal)
Includes index.
Issued in print and electronic formats.
ISBN 978-0-7787-4669-0 (hardcover).--
ISBN 978-0-7787-4682-9 (softcover).--
ISBN 978-1-4271-2066-3 (HTML)

        1. Bamboo--Juvenile literature. 2. Bamboo--Ecology--
Juvenile literature. 3. Plant communities--Juvenile literature.
4. Forest ecology--Juvenile literature. I. Title.

QK495.G74H833 2018   j584'.922   C2017-907625-6
                                                            C2017-907626-4

Library of Congress Cataloging-in-Publication Data

Names: Hudak, Heather C., 1975- author.
Title: Bamboo forest research journal / Heather Hudak.
Description: New York, New York : Crabtree Publishing Company,
    [2018] | Series: Ecosystems research journal | Includes index.
Identifiers: LCCN 2017057530 (print) | LCCN 2017061593 (ebook)
    ISBN 9781427120663 (Electronic HTML) |
    ISBN 9780778746690 (reinforced library binding : alk. paper)
    ISBN 9780778746829 (pbk. : alk. paper)
Subjects: LCSH: Forests and forestry--China--Chun'an Xian-
    -Juvenile literature. | Bamboo--Ecology--Juvenile literature.
    | Giant panda--Juvenile literature. | Chun'an Xian (China)--
    Juvenile literature.
Classification: LCC SD221 (ebook) | LCC SD221 .H84 2018
    (print) | DDC 577.3--dc23
LC record available at https://lccn.loc.gov/2017057530

Crabtree Publishing Company
www.crabtreebooks.com   1-800-387-7650

Printed in the U.S.A./022018/CG20171220

Published in Canada
Crabtree Publishing
616 Welland Ave.
St. Catharines, Ontario
L2M 5V6

Published in the United States
Crabtree Publishing
PMB 59051
350 Fifth Avenue, 59th Floor
New York, New York 10118

Published in the United Kingdom
Crabtree Publishing
Maritime House
Basin Road North, Hove
BN41 1WR

Published in Australia
Crabtree Publishing
3 Charles Street
Coburg North
VIC, 3058

Contents

Mission to the Shunan Bamboo Forest

Time to pack my bug spray and raincoat! I am off to the Shunan Bamboo Forest in China. Bamboo forests are places where the temperatures and landscapes are perfect for large amounts of bamboo to grow. I have wanted to visit a bamboo forest ever since I became a **wildlife biologist**. I am going to China with an organization called Friends of the Forests. They want to know how **deforestation**, tourism, and **climate change** are affecting bamboo. We will also study the animal species that rely on bamboo to survive. There is not a lot of research on bamboo forests, so I'm hoping to learn as much as I can!

The Shunan Bamboo Forest is sometimes called the Shunan Bamboo Sea because it looks like a sea of bamboo from above.

There are more than 300 species of bamboo in China. Bamboo covers about 7,700 square miles (20,000 square kilometers) of the country. This represents about 20 percent of the world's total bamboo.

I hoped to see a Chinese muntjac. These deer bark like a dog.

What I find so interesting about bamboo is that it is actually a grass. Some types of bamboo are so tall, they are often called trees. Bamboo mainly grows in forests in Southeast Asia, Japan, and China. Shunan Bamboo Forest is one of the biggest bamboo forests in China. Bamboo grows best in places with **tropical**, **subtropical**, and mild climates. The average temperature in Shunan is about 60 °F (15.5 °C). It is quite cloudy and humid most of the year. I chose to visit in July, which is the hottest, wettest month of the year. There will be lots of plants and animals for me to study. Shunan is home to some species that are not be found anywhere else on Earth!

Shunan Bamboo Forest

Min River

Tuo River

Yangtze River

SICHUAN PROVINCE

Chengdu

Leshan

Yibin

Qinglong Lake

Sea in the Sea

Tianbao Village

Jade Corridor

Wangyou Valley

Xianyu Cave

Guanyun Pavilion

Yangtze River

Shunan Bamboo Forest covers about 46 square miles (120 square kilometers) of China's Sichuan Province.

5

Field Journal: Day 1

Chengdu

I started my trip in Chengdu, the capital of China's Sichuan Province. Chengdu is located on the Chengdu Plain. The plain is a large, flat area of land made up of **sediment** deposited from nearby rivers. The Yangtze River and its **tributaries**, the Min and Tuo rivers, run through the area. I arrived in Chengdu on a morning flight and met up with the rest of the research group at our hotel. We wanted to learn more about the region and what makes it special before heading to Shunan Bamboo Forest.

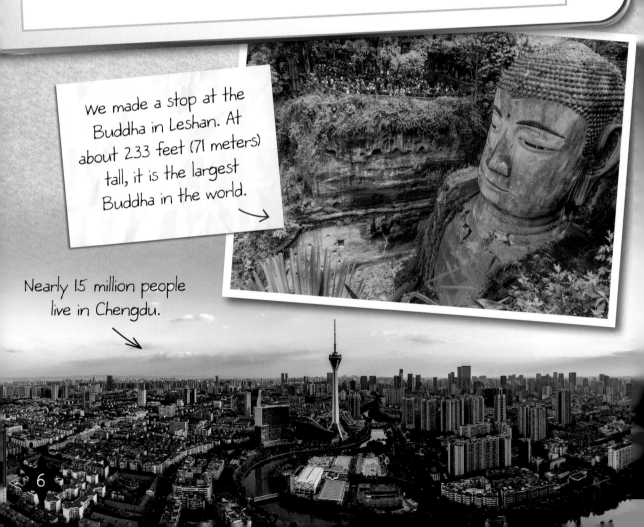

We made a stop at the Buddha in Leshan. At about 233 feet (71 meters) tall, it is the largest Buddha in the world. →

Nearly 15 million people live in Chengdu. ↘

Our first visit was to the ancient Dujiangyan **irrigation** system. An archaeologist showed us around the site. It was built more than 2,000 years ago and is still used today. It is almost perfectly preserved. The irrigation system is very important for water **conservation** in the area. It controls the flow of water from the Min River, which stops it from flooding Chengdu when the water level is high. The system also works in reverse to bring water to farmers' fields during **droughts**.

The Dujiangyan irrigation system ←

natstat STATUS REPORT ST456/part B

Name: Pangolin (Pholidota)

Threats:
Poaching

Description:
Pangolins are covered in hard scales and have sharp claws. They eat only ants and termites. Pangolins are 1–3 feet (0.3–1 m) long (not including their tail) and weigh 10–60 pounds (4.5–27 kg). The word pangolin means "rolling over" in the Malay language. Pangolins roll into a ball when they are afraid. People hunt them for their meat, scales, skin, and organs. Sightings in China are so rare, there is no accurate count of their numbers.

Status: 4 species are **vulnerable**, 2 species are **endangered**, and 2 species are critically endangered

Attach photograph here ➡

Field Journal: Day 2

Chengdu Research Base of Giant Panda Breeding

Today, we visited the Chengdu Research Base of Giant Panda Breeding. Pandas are only found in China and are considered a national treasure. In the wild, they are found in China's Sichuan, Shaanxi, and Gansu provinces. There are fewer than 2,000 pandas left, and about 70 percent of them live in Sichuan Province. We caught the bus right after breakfast so we could get to the center early in the day, when the weather was still cool. Pandas are less active when it is hot outside. We took a walk along some of the outdoor trails and saw pandas playing and eating.

Male pandas can grow as tall as 6 feet (1.83 meters) and weigh up to 220 pounds (100 kilograms). Bamboo makes up 99 percent of their diet. They eat as much as 84 pounds (38 kilograms) of bamboo each day.

Chengdu Research Base of Giant Panda Breeding

Pandas are an important part of the **ecosystems** where they live. They spread plant seeds in their droppings as they move about. This helps forests grow and thrive. Pandas have been threatened since the 1960s. The bamboo forests they call home are being cut down to make way for cities and towns, and people hunt them even though it is illegal. Scientists at the center are working to increase the number of pandas in the world. They have the world's largest **artificial** breeding program. More than 100 pandas have been born at the center since it opened in 1987. Conservation efforts are working. The status of pandas has changed from endangered to vulnerable.

↑ Inside, baby pandas were sleeping. They were wrapped in pink and blue blankets to keep them warm.

Breeding programs are just one way to help pandas. The Chinese government and many other organizations focus on protecting the panda's habitat, too. This helps other at-risk animals in the area, such as the pangolin, the golden snub-nosed monkey, and the lesser bamboo bat.

Field Journal: Day 3

Chengdu to Shunan Bamboo Forest

After two days in Chengdu, it was time to head to the Shunan Bamboo Forest. We caught a bus heading southwest to Yibin. We checked into a guesthouse near the western gates of the forest entrance in Wanling. I couldn't wait to get to the Bamboo Forest Museum. It is the only museum of its kind in China. A guide took us through the museum's six display halls to view artifacts made of bamboo. Bamboo is hollow and can float. It can be split, shaped, and bent. This makes it ideal for building large structures such as houses and bridges. Many people also use it to build furniture, hats, baskets, and more. Some artifacts at the museum date back more than 7,000 years.

Bamboo can be used to make everything from chopsticks to boats, like this one I saw on my way to the museum.

I was astonished to learn that bamboo is more than twice as strong as steel!

Bamboo is strong enough to be used in building houses.

We walked through the bamboo garden next. We saw examples of the 58 different types of bamboo that grow in Shunan, including nan, concave, mao, and fish pole. Bamboo forests are very different from hardwood forests, where it can take hundreds of years for trees to grow big and tall. Because it is a grass, bamboo can grow very quickly. Some types of bamboo can grow up to 40 feet (12 meters) in less than two months. I got to see bamboo shoots at different stages in their life cycle. This helped me understand how bamboo forests grow so quickly.

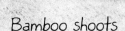

Bamboo shoots

The Growth of Bamboo

Height

40 feet (12 meters)

20 feet (6 meters)

Young bamboo shoot underground growth

Young bamboo shoot above ground growth

18 days   28 days   36 days   44 days   56 days

Time

Field Journal: Day 4

Overnight in Wangyou Valley

I had heard about a place called Wangyou Valley. Legend has it that walking around this beautiful valley will make you forget your worries. Many farmers in this area are concerned about the disappearing bamboo forests. They make a living growing bamboo. I met a farmer who took me on a walk along a stream to his bamboo groves. Along the way, we stopped to talk to some of the other farmers.

A bamboo farmer in Sichuan →

natstat STATUS REPORT ST456/part B

Name: Sichuan partridge
(Tetraophasis szechenyii)

Threats:
Hunting and habitat loss

Description:
The Sichuan partridge lives only in China. It is mainly found in hardwood forests. Much of its natural habitat has been turned into farmland. Not much is known about the Sichuan partridge, so it is difficult to come up with a plan to protect them.

Numbers: 1,000–1,500

Status: Endangered

Attach photograph here

Forests of hardwood trees and bamboo that have been cut down often only grow back as hardwood forests. ↓

The Chinese government created laws to stop too many hardwood trees from being cut down to be used as timber. Because of this, farmers started to cut down more bamboo instead. They relied on it for most of their income. They grew more bamboo to make more money and stopped growing other plants. This led to less **biodiversity** in some areas. Animals that relied on other plants had to **adapt** to this lack of food or look for other places to live. Some species died off.

The Rise in Bamboo Forest Deforestation

100 million stalks lost — Year

Bars shown for years: 1978, 1988, 1992, 1994, 1998, 2002, 2012

Field Journal: Day 5

Wangyou Valley Papermaking

This morning, my group met a family that lives along the riverbank. They make paper by hand from bamboo. They showed us how to do it. They let the bamboo grow for five months, then cut it into 5-foot (1.5-meter) sections. The pieces are soaked for several months. When it is soft enough, it is beaten into a pulp, or paste. Some families use a stone wheel powered by a cow, but this family has a machine with a gas engine.

In a 10-hour shift, a family can make about 2,400 sheets of bamboo paper. ↓

The family shared their breakfast with us. It was a type of wonton called Hóng yóu chǎoshǒu—a square of pastry filled with meat and vegetables. We dunked it in chili oil before eating it. It was so spicy that it made my eyes water!

I helped the family place the pulp into molds. They use a hand-operated press, which is a machine that squeezes out all the water. Then we hung each sheet on a line to dry. While we worked, the family talked about some of the issues threatening their way of life. Many local people rely on bamboo for much more than just their income. They use it to build their homes, furniture, food, cooking and eating utensils, fishing gear, and more. Some even sell bamboo handicrafts, such as hats, jewelry, and flutes, to tourists.

The family uses powder from a plant called sweet hibiscus to help the paper keep its form.

About 57 billion pairs of disposable chopsticks are made in China each year. Nearly 13 million square feet (1.2 million square meters) of bamboo forest are cut down to make them.

Many local families make bamboo hats to keep the sun off their heads. They also sell them to tourists.

15

Field Journal: Day 6

Guanyun Pavilion and Jade Corridor

We were close by the Guanyun Pavilion, which is famous for "cloud viewing." I couldn't resist a quick visit to this mountainous area. The view from the top was amazing. Everything was covered in a foggy mist, and it felt like I was standing in a sea of clouds. Tall bamboo swayed all around me, and I could see for miles.

Sightings

I spotted a masked palm civet climbing a tree. They look like cats, but they're more closely related to weasels and mongooses. Their numbers are decreasing due to habitat loss.

Masked palm civet →

↑ It was cold and damp at the top, and I was glad I packed my raincoat.

Jade Corridor pathway

There was still plenty of time to explore more of the forest. I had heard a lot about the Jade Corridor. This is a beautiful red sandstone pathway with tall bamboo forming a canopy over the top. I tried to keep my eyes open for the endangered red panda. It's very rare to see these small, bear-like mammals in nature. They are often captured and sold to zoos for display. Many organizations are looking for ways to stop people from hunting red pandas. They also try to protect the red panda's habitat. The World Wildlife Fund (WWF) works with local people to help them find other sources of income, such as tourism.

natstat STATUS REPORT ST456/part B

Name: Red panda (Ailurus fulgens)

Description:
The red panda is a bamboo–eating animal that is slightly larger than a house cat. It is known for its distinctive reddish–brown fur. Red pandas are found mostly in temperate forests. About 50 percent of them live in the eastern Himalayas. The loss of bamboo to eat and the trees they nest in are causing their numbers to decline.

Threats:
Hunting, habitat loss, and getting caught in traps meant for other animals

Numbers: Less than 10,000

Status: Endangered

Attach photograph here ➡

17

Field Journal: Day 7

Sea in the Sea

As we continued our trek, we came upon a vast body of water in the middle of the forest. This is known as the "Sea in the Sea," because it looks like a sea in the middle of the Shunan Bamboo Sea. The lake wasn't always there. The area was once a valley in the Zhuhai Mountains. It filled with water after a **dam** was built in 1998. Dams are built in China to prevent regular flooding and to create electricity. They can be useful, but they also change the landscape. They have a big impact on the people and animals that live in an area.

Sightings

I was lucky to spot a lesser bamboo bat, since these bats are really tiny. They live inside hollow bamboo stems and only come out at night to feast on insects.

Lesser bamboo bat

At first I thought the lake water was dirty because it was green, but the color is actually the reflection of the bamboo.

The Yangtze River overflows during the monsoon season. It can cause terrible flooding. In 1998, flooding killed thousands of people and left 14 million homeless. Millions of acres of land were destroyed. Plants help slow the flow of rainwater, which can prevent flooding. Deforestation by humans made the floods worse. Two government programs were started in 2000 to bring forests and grasslands back to help reduce flooding. One is called the Natural Forest Conservation Program, and the other program pays farmers to convert their farmland.

Flooding is common along the Yangtze River. It can destroy homes and farmland.

During the 1998 floods, about 21 million acres (8.5 million hectares) ended up underwater. Another 11 million acres (4.4 million hectares) of crops were destroyed.

Field Journal: Day 8

Xianyu Cave

This morning, we got up early to visit Xianyu Cave. Lots of tourists were already there when we arrived. The cave was more like a corridor along a cliff on the side of a mountain. We walked inside and were amazed by the Buddhist statues we saw. I noticed that some of them were broken. A guide explained that they had been damaged by people and weather over the years. From the cave, there were amazing views of the forest below. But I saw someone tossing trash on the ground. Another person was walking off the trail to pick some flowers. These activities damage the environment and could even harm the wildlife.

I rode a cable car to reach Xianyu Cave. ↓

Sightings

I smelled a strong, flowery scent. I looked around and noticed plum blossoms growing nearby.

Plum blossoms ↙

Shunan Bamboo Forest faces some big challenges because of tourism. The government of China has made laws to help protect **cultural relics**. Action is taken against people who damage or steal relics. Some relics are built inside caves or into the sides of mountains. In the past, they were often destroyed to build new structures. Today, China takes steps to avoid building on the site of relics that cannot be moved. The government is also making more natural protection zones. These green spaces and ecosystems cannot be used for human construction.

Statues and other relics in the bamboo forests of China are now protected by law.

严禁烟火
48

natstat STATUS REPORT ST456/part B

Name: Golden snub-nosed monkey
(Rhinopithecus roxellana)

Threats:
Hunting, habitat loss

Description:

Golden snub-nosed monkeys are known for their flat, fleshy noses and long, yellowish-red coats. They live high in mountainous forests in western-central China.
They are social animals that often live in large groups. Golden snub-nosed monkeys are hunted for their fur and meat, as well as their bones, which are thought to have medicinal properties.

Numbers: 8,000 to 20,000

Status: Endangered

Attach photograph here ➡

Field Journal: Day 9

Fairy Lake and Tianbao Village

After visiting Xianyu Cave, we made our way to the top of the hill to see Fairy Lake. The water here is completely clear, and the reflection of the bamboo trees in the water makes it look like a painting. Growing more beautiful forests like this one can help slow down the effects of climate change. Like other plants, bamboo takes in and stores carbon as it grows. Carbon is a chemical that plays a part in increasing Earth's temperature. The warming of Earth is contributing to the problems of climate change. Bamboo grows quickly. Scientists hope that growing more bamboo forests will mean less carbon in the air and more carbon stored in the trees.

Sightings

I saw a bamboo rat climbing a tree. They mainly eat bamboo shoots but will also search on the ground for fruits and seeds.

← Bamboo rat

We took bamboo rafts across Fairy Lake to reach Tianbao Village. In the mid-1800s, the Qing Dynasty government carved this village into a cliff ledge nearly 3,300 feet (more than 1,000 meters) above the ground. It was built to defend against attacks. Green bamboo creates a natural screen that hides the village from view. Rare pedestal rocks that stand 33 feet (10 meters) high surround the village. They look like mushrooms with a tall stem and a large top. They get their unique shape from **weathering** and **erosion**.

Bamboo raft ↙

Pedestal rock ↓

There are a total of **58** types of bamboo in the Shunan Bamboo Forest.

Rainbow Waterfall

Making our way to Rainbow Waterfall, we noticed some exposed bamboo roots along the lake. We stopped to take a closer look. I had heard that bamboo roots can help keep soil from eroding in places where logging has cleared the trees. Looking at the ball of long roots, I could see why. Tree roots do not hold soil in place after a forest has been logged. But bamboo roots keep growing even after the plant is cut down. They help hold onto the soil.

I watched the water tumble down over the 650-foot (200-meter) drop. I could see rainbows in the water as it splashed down. ↘

The roots of a single bamboo plant can hold as much as 212 cubic feet (6 cubic meters) of soil!

We met up with a conservation biologist from a nearby university. The biologist told me that today's bamboo forests could be wiped out by the end of the century because of climate change. At the same time, climate change is making some other places warm enough for new bamboo forests to grow. If people work to protect existing forests, and plant bamboo in new areas, this important plant can be saved from extinction.

I thought I saw a leaf move on a nearby tree, but there wasn't a breeze. I got up close to take a look, and I saw some stick bugs. They are hard to see because they look like bamboo.

↙ Stick bug

↖ If these forests die, the animals that eat mainly bamboo will die out too, unless they can adapt.

25

Qinglong Lake

On the last day of our research trip, we wanted to see more birds. We heard that Qinglong Lake was a great place to go bird watching, so we headed there. Many **migratory** birds are found there, including ducks that spend the winter there. We hired boatmen to pull us along the lake on rafts as we looked for birds. Our main goal was to see the pheasant-tailed jacana, as well as the black drongo and the Chinese sparrowhawk. I also hoped to see some of the birds that are only found in this part of the world. I was lucky to spot two of them—the Chinese bulbul and the Chinese blackbird!

Black drongo ↗

Chinese sparrowhawk ↗

Out of nowhere, I heard a loud, high-pitched sound, and I nearly fell off my raft! I looked up and saw a Sichuan treecreeper sitting in a tree. Not much is known about these small birds. It was a rare find!

26

I asked our boatman if he had ever seen bamboo when it flowers. He shook his head and said he hoped he never would. Once it flowers and spreads new seeds, the old bamboo dies off. An entire forest can flower at the same time, killing off all the bamboo in a habitat. It can take 15 to 20 years to grow a new forest. Wildlife that needs bamboo to survive must adapt or migrate. This was easier before bamboo forests were cut down to make way for roads and towns. Today, it is not so easy. Many animals starve.

Most species of bamboo flower once every 60–130 years.

→

natstat STATUS REPORT ST456/part B

Name: Pheasant-tailed jacana
(Hydrophasianus chirurgus)

Threats:
Habitat loss

Numbers: Unknown

Status: Declining

Description:

These colorful wading birds live mostly in lakes, ponds, and swamps. They eat mainly insects and small animals, such as crabs and worms, that they pick off plants. The feathers of pheasant-tailed jacanas change with the seasons. In breeding season, they grow very long tail feathers.

Attach photograph here ➡

Final Report

REPORT TO:
FRIENDS OF THE FORESTS

OBSERVATIONS

Spending time in the Shunan Bamboo Forest has helped me realize how important it is to protect bamboo plants. Of the 1,200 bamboo species in the world, about 50 percent are facing extinction by the year 2070 due to deforestation. I have learned that bamboo is an important habitat and food source for many unique species. I have also seen how people use it in their daily lives.

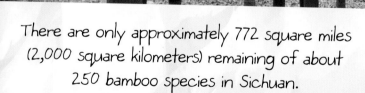

There are only approximately 772 square miles (2,000 square kilometers) remaining of about 250 bamboo species in Sichuan.

Bamboo releases 30 percent more oxygen than other plants.

FUTURE CONCERNS

Deforestation is just one threat bamboo forests face. Climate change is also a problem. Bamboo can only grow in certain climates. As Earth's temperature rises, there are fewer places with ideal growing conditions for bamboo. Bamboo is the main source of food for many animal species. Without bamboo, they may become extinct. The local people also rely on bamboo to make their living, too.

CONSERVATION PROJECTS

The government of China and international groups such as Conservation International are working to protect bamboo forests from further destruction. The government started a conservation program in 2020 that aims to maintain biodiversity. Some organizations have reforestation programs. They plant new bamboo grasses in places where bamboo has been cut down. Other groups are researching ways to protect areas that may become suitable for bamboo to grow in the future. Some groups, such as a conservation organization called the World Wildlife Fund, focus on protecting specific animal species, such as giant pandas, from the threats of bamboo loss.

Today, there are 67 panda reserves in China, as well as breeding programs like the one at the Chengdu Research Base of Giant Panda Breeding.

29

Your Turn

✸ This journal is a work of fiction. It is based on real facts and research, though. Read books, watch documentaries, and look online to learn more about bamboo forests. Can you find evidence to support the facts in this journal? What other facts can you find about bamboo forests? Write a journal entry sharing this information.

✸ Go for a walk in your community to learn more about the different species living there. Makes notes, draw pictures, and take photos of any plants or animals you see. Take notice of any threats to nature that you observe. Is there trash on the sidewalk? Are any new roads being built? Talk to your neighbors, teachers, and family to find out how these threats have an impact on them, too.

✸ Giant pandas, golden snub-nosed monkeys, and red pandas are just a few of the animals that rely on bamboo for survival. Research other animals that live in bamboo forests. What impact does habitat loss or poaching have on these species?

✸ Many organizations are working to help protect bamboo forests. Imagine you work for one of them, and you have been given the job of getting the word out about your work. Write a web page or brochure about your organization and how people can get involved.

Learning More

BOOKS

Ancient China Inside Out by Kelly Spence (Crabtree Publishing, 2017)

Bamboo by Ideals Publications (Rourke Publishing, 2011)

Camp Panda: Helping Cubs Return to the Wild by Catherine Thimmesh (HMH Books for Young Readers, 2018)

Red Pandas: Shy Forest Dwellers by Claire Johnston (CreateSpace Independent Publishing Platform, 2014)

WEBSITES

www.panda.org.cn/english/
Learn all about giant pandas, the threats they face, and programs to protect them.

http://whc.unesco.org/en/list/1001
Find out more about the Dujiangyan Irrigation System and UNESCO World Heritage Site.

www.chinascenic.com/magazine/the-world-of-bamboo-212.html
Visit this website for information, images, and graphs about bamboo and how it is used in China.

Glossary & Index

adapt   to change over time to become better suited to an ecosystem

artificial   something that is made by humans

biodiversity   the variety of species in a habitat or environment

climate change   a change in the normal weather in an area over time that is caused by pollution and other human actions

conservation   the careful use of resources

cultural relics   places of historical and cultural importance

dam   a structure that prevents water from flowing

deforestation   the cutting down of forests and woodlands

droughts   long periods without rainfall

ecosystem   a community of plants, animals, and their environments

endangered   at risk of becoming extinct

erosion   a process in which soil and rocks are worn away by wind and water over time

irrigation   a system used to supply water to crops to help them grow

migratory   describing something that moves to a new habitat for a period of time, usually when the seasons change

poaching   hunting wild animals illegally

sediment   dirt, soil, and sand that is carried by water and is deposited on the land or at the bottom of the river

subtropical   describing areas next to tropical areas, which are slightly cooler and less damp

tributaries   rivers that flow into a river or lake

tropical   describing areas that are typically hot and damp

vulnerable   at risk of becoming endangered

weathering   the act of wearing something away and changing the way it looks

wildlife biologist   a scientist who studies animals